The Versatile Apple

Delightful to behold
Easy to prepare
Delicious to eat —
 and good for all!

～ Enjoy ～

Main Dishes —
  Caraway Pork Chops   1
  Cabbage Beef Casserole   2
  Curried Apples & Shrimp   3
  Meatloaf   4
  Spareribs & Apples   5
  Stir-fried Chicken   6
  Stir-fried Scallops   7
Side Dishes —
  Apple-filled Squash   8
  Hot Potato Salad   9
  Noodle Casserole   10
  Sweet Potatoes & Apples   11
Salads —
  Apple Slaw   12
  Dutch Apple   13
  Ginger Apple   14
  Chilled Vegetables   14
  Tropical Chicken   15
  Waldorf   13
Breads —
  Apple Banana   16
  Apple Cheese   17
  Quick Muffins   18

Desserts
- Apple Crisp — 19
- Apple Pan Dowdy — 20
- Apple Pie — 21
- Applesauce — 22
- Raspberry Applesauce — 23
- Applesauce Meringue — 24
- Apple Squares — 25
- Baked Apples — 26
- Apples Meringue — 26
- Apple Rings — 27
- Date & Apple Squares — 28
- Easy Apple Cake — 29
- Scones — 30
- Topping — 28

Extras
- Apple Butter — 31
- Apple Dip — 32
- Fritters — 33
- Honey Apples — 33
- Pancakes — 34
- Peanut Butter & Apples — 35
- Relish — 32
- Stuffing — 36

Jeanne Amero

Wellspring
York, Pennsylvania

printed on recycled paper

calligraphy by p. dutery

Caraway Pork Chops

Serves 6

- 2 medium onions, thinly sliced
- 3 apples, peeled and thinly sliced
- 2 tbsp. honey
- 2 tsp. caraway seeds
- 6 ½-inch pork chops
- garlic salt and pepper
- Dijon mustard

Preheat oven 350°.
Layer onions and apples in the bottom of a shallow baking dish. Drizzle honey on top and sprinkle with 1 tsp. caraway seeds.

Prepare chops by sprinkling them with garlic salt and pepper and spreading mustard on them. Place chops on apples and sprinkle with remaining 1 tsp. caraway seeds.
Cover and bake 1 hour.

Cabbage Casserole

Serves 6

- 1 medium onion, chopped
- 1 stalk celery, chopped
- 3 tbsp. margarine
- 3/4 lb. lean ground beef
- 1/2 tsp. salt
- 1 medium cabbage, shredded
- 2 apples, sliced thin

Preheat oven 350°.
In skillet, saute onion and celery in margarine 2 minutes. Add beef and salt and stir another 2 minutes. Spread half the cabbage in 2 quart baking dish and cover with half the apples and all the meat mixture. Add remaining cabbage and apple slices. Cover and bake 1 hour. Nice with mashed potatoes or noodles.

Curried Apples & Shrimp

Serves 4

- 1 medium onion, chopped
- 2 stalks celery, chopped
- 4 tbsp. butter or margarine
- 2 apples, sliced
- 3/4 tsp. curry powder
- 2 tsp. flour
- 3/4 cup water
- 1 chicken bouillon cube
- 3/4 lb. medium shrimp, shelled and cleaned

Saute onion and celery in butter for 2 minutes. Add apple slices and saute another minute. Blend in curry and flour, add bouillon cube and water, stirring until well blended. Add shrimp, cover and simmer for 3 minutes, or until shrimp is no longer translucent. Good with rice.

Apple Meatloaf

Serves 4

1 lb. lean ground beef
1 apple, cored and chopped
1 medium onion, chopped
½ tsp. garlic salt
⅛ tsp. pepper

1 or 2 slices bread

Preheat oven 350°.
Combine all ingredients except bread. Soak bread in cold water, squeeze out moisture, shred and add. Place in loaf pan and bake 25-30 minutes. Or...form into patties, roll in bread crumbs and pan fry, or broil.

Apples are low in sodium and cholesterol, and high in vitamin A and C — and they contain a calorie content ranging from 75 to 120 calories per apple.

Spareribs & Apples

Serves 4

5 lbs. meaty spareribs
3 tbsp. butter
pepper
1 qt. sauerkraut, rinsed
2 onions, sliced
1 carrot, grated
3 apples, sliced
1½ cups dry white wine

Preheat oven 350°. In skillet, lightly brown spareribs in butter. Sprinkle with pepper. In separate bowl, mix together sauerkraut, onions and carrots. Place half this mixture in baking dish. Add half the apple slices and all the spareribs. Cover with remaining sauerkraut mixture, apple slices and wine. Cover and bake 1 hour 45 minutes.
Nice with mashed potatoes.

Stir-fried Chicken & Apples

Serves 4-5

2 whole chicken breasts, skinned and deboned
1/3 cup honey
2 tsp. curry powder
2 apples, peeled and sliced
3 tbsp. oil
1 stalk celery, sliced
1/4 cup raisins
3 tbsp. chopped parsley

Cut chicken into cubes and place in bowl. Combine honey and curry and mix thru chicken. Stir in apple slices.

Heat oil in heavy skillet over high heat. Saute celery for one minute. Add apple mixture and stir-fry 3-4 minutes....just until chicken is no longer pink. Add raisins and parsley, stir well and serve over rice.

Stir-fried Scallops & Apples

Serves 4

- 2 stalks celery
- 1 lb. scallops
- 2 apples
- 3 tbsp. margarine
- 1 lemon

Coarsely cut celery, and slice scallops. Peel and quarter apples. Heat margarine in heavy skillet over high heat and stir-fry celery for 2 minutes. Add scallops, sprinkling with juice from half the lemon. Coarsely cut apple pieces into mixture, stirring constantly, for another 2-3 minutes, adding more margarine, if needed. Sprinkle with juice from remaining half of lemon, and serve.

Due to their natural sugar content, apples supply us with quick energy.

Apple-filled Acorn Squash

    3 acorn squash

Combine:

    2 apples, chopped
    ½ cup chopped walnuts
    1 tbsp. grated orange peel
    ½ cup brown sugar
    2 tbsp. margarine, melted

Preheat oven 350°.
Cut squash in half lengthwise and scrape out seeds. Place cut side down in baking dish and bake for 25 minutes.
Mix the other ingredients. Turn cut side up, fill with apple mix and continue baking for 20 minutes, or until squash is tender.

Shiny red or yellow apples nestled in freshly cut greens make an easy and attractive Christmas decoration.

Hot Potato Salad

Serves 6

3 cups cooked cubed potatoes
1½ cups coarsely chopped apples
10 slices bacon
½ cup chopped onion
½ cup chopped celery
1½ tbsp. flour
¾ cup apple juice...or water
⅓ cup vinegar
⅓ cup sugar

In skillet, cook bacon. Remove and drain. Pour off all but 3 tbsp. bacon fat, add onion and celery and stir-fry 1-2 minutes. Blend in flour. Add juice and vinegar, stirring until mixture thickens. Add sugar. Preheat oven 350°. Place potatoes, apples and crumbled bacon in greased 1½ quart casserole. Add skillet mixture, mixing lightly. Cover and bake 30 minutes.

Apples & Noodles

   2 cups cooked noodles
   2 apples, peeled and sliced
   cinnamon
   4 tbsp. brown sugar
   4 tbsp. butter

Preheat oven 350°.
Place half the noodles and apples in a buttered baking dish. Sprinkle with half the brown sugar and cinnamon. Dot with half the butter. Repeat. Cover and bake 30 minutes. Stir well before serving.

There are over 7,000 varieties of apples grown in the United States. About 18 varieties are used by apple growers for marketing purposes.

Sweet Potatoes & Apples

Serves 4-6

2 cups boiled, skinned sweet potatoes
2 apples, peeled
½ cup brown sugar
4 tbsp. butter
½ tsp. salt

Preheat oven 350°.
Slice cooked potatoes and apples ¼ to ½ inch thick. Place half of each in buttered baking dish. Sprinkle with half the sugar, salt and dot with half the butter. Repeat.
Cover and bake 40 minutes.

Variation: Add ½ cup chopped nuts and/or tablespoon of grated orange rind.

Three medium apples equal 1 lb. or 3 cups when sliced or chopped.

Apple Slaw

Serves 4-6

2 apples, thinly sliced
2 tbsp. lemon juice
3 cups shredded cabbage
1 stalk celery, chopped
1 carrot, grated
1 medium onion, thinly sliced

½ cup sour cream
¼ cup mayonnaise
3/4 tsp. celery salt

Sprinkle sliced apples with lemon juice. Mix with cabbage, celery, carrot and onion. Combine sour cream, mayonnaise and celery salt. Toss with apple mixture and serve.

Lemon juice keeps apples from discoloring.

Dutch Apple Salad

Serves 4-6

1 cup cooked, diced ham
3/4 cup cooked, diced potatoes
2 apples, peeled, cored and chopped
2 hard-cooked eggs, chopped
2 pickles, chopped
1/4 cup Italian or Buttermilk dressing

Combine ingredients and serve on lettuce leaves.

Waldorf Salad is traditionally a mix of coarsely chopped nuts, apples, celery and raisins combined with mayonnaise.
For a change, substitute fresh chunks of pineapple for the celery, and buttermilk dressing instead of mayonnaise.

Ginger Apple Salad

Serves 4-5

   8 apples, cored and chopped
   1 tbsp. grated ginger root
   1 cup chopped celery
   ½ cup raisins
   ½ cup chopped walnuts
   2 tbsp. honey
   ⅓ cup orange juice

Combine above ingredients and chill. Serve on lettuce leaves. Nice, garnished with slices of orange and mint leaves.

Chilled Vegetables & Apples

Combine cooked vegetables such as green beans, carrots, brussels sprouts, cauliflower, etc. with a few chopped green onions and a chopped apple. Add some Italian dressing, chill and serve.

Tropical Chicken Salad

Serves 6

2 cups white meat chicken, cooked and cubed
2 apples, peeled and diced
1 cup pineapple chunks
1/3 cup chopped almonds
1/2 cup shredded coconut
1/4 cup white raisins...optional
3 tbsp. chopped chutney
2 tsp. curry powder
3/4 cup mayonnaise

Combine all but last 3 ingredients. In separate bowl, combine chutney, curry and mayonnaise. Stir into chicken mixture, and serve on watercress or lettuce leaves, with slices of avocado.

Once cut, certain varities of apples, such as Golden Delicious and Cortland, remain white much longer than others. Your supplier will know.

Apple Banana Bread

½ cup butter, softened
1 cup sugar, half brown, half granulated
2 eggs
3 tbsp. sour cream
1 banana, mashed
1 tsp. vanilla
2 cups flour
1 tsp. baking powder
1 tsp. baking soda
½ tsp. cinnamon
2 apples, cored and chopped
½ cup chopped walnuts

Preheat oven 350°. Cream butter and sugars and beat in eggs. Stir in sour cream, banana and vanilla. In separate bowl, combine flour, baking powder, soda and cinnamon. Gradually add to butter mixture. Gently stir in apples and nuts. Spoon into greased bread pan and bake 1 hour.

Apple Cheese Bread

- ½ cup butter or margarine
- ⅔ cup sugar
- 2 eggs
- 1 apple, peeled and chopped
- ½ cup grated sharp Cheddar cheese
- ⅓ cup chopped walnuts
- 2 cups flour
- 1 tsp. baking powder
- ½ tsp. baking soda
- ½ tsp. salt

Preheat oven 350°. Cream butter and sugar, beating until light. Beat in eggs, one at a time. Stir in apples, cheese and nuts. In separate bowl, combine flour, baking powder, soda and salt. Gradually and gently stir into apple mixture. Pour into greased loaf pan and bake 1 hour. Cool 10 minutes before serving.

Quick Applesauce Muffins

2 cups Bisquick
1/4 cup sugar
1 tsp. cinnamon
1/2 cup applesauce
1/4 cup milk
1 egg
2 tbsp. cooking oil

1/4 cup sugar
1/4 tsp. cinnamon
2 tbsp. butter or margarine, melted

Preheat oven 400°. Combine Bisquick, 1/4 cup sugar and 1 tsp. cinnamon. Add applesauce, milk, egg and oil and beat vigorously for 30 seconds. Fill greased muffin pans 2/3 full and bake 12-15 minutes. Cool slightly and remove from pans. Mix remaining sugar and cinnamon. Dip tops of muffins in melted butter, then in sugar-cinnamon. Makes 12.

Most apples fall into two categories — eating apples and cooking apples. As few are good for both purposes, ask your provider.

Apple Crisp

Serves 8

    5 apples, sliced and peeled
    1 cup brown sugar
    3/4 cup Quaker Oats
    3/4 cup flour
    1 tsp. cinnamon
    1 tsp. nutmeg
    1 stick butter, softened
    1/4 cup apple juice... or water

Preheat oven 375.° Put half the apples in a greased 9"x9" pan. Blend together remaining ingredients...except juice, and crumble half the flour mixture over the apples. Cover with remaining apples and flour mixture. Pour juice over top. Bake 35 minutes. Great with vanilla ice cream.

Apple Pan Dowdy

½ cup brown sugar
¼ cup chopped walnuts
¼ cup raisins
3 cups apples, sliced
¼ cup butter, softened
⅔ cup sugar
1 egg, beaten
2¼ cups flour
4 tsp. baking powder
½ tsp. salt
1 cup milk

In bottom of buttered baking dish, sprinkle some brown sugar, nuts and raisins. Layer in apples and remaining brown sugar. Preheat oven 350°. Cream butter, add sugar gradually, then add beaten egg. Sift flour, baking powder and salt. Combine creamed mix, dry ingredients and milk alternately till smooth. Pour batter over apples. Bake 35-40 minutes. Turn over on plate with apple side up. Serve with topping.

Firm, tart, juicy apples are best for baking. Some areas are blessed with many varieties to choose from. Wherever you live there will be a preferred "pie" apple. Ask your supplier.

Basic Apple Pie

Make pastry for a 2-crust 9" pie.
Mix 1 tsp. cinnamon thru 3/4 cup sugar.
Slice 6 or 7...peeled or unpeeled...apples and mix with cinnamon-sugar. Pile into a pastry-lined pie pan, dot with butter and cover with slitted top crust. Bake 425° for about 50 minutes.

Delightful variation: Mix apples with a combination of:
- 1/2 cup brown sugar
- 1/4 cup honey
- 1/2 cup raisins
- 1/2 cup broken pecans...or walnuts

Dot with butter and bake as above.
If apples are very juicy, add 1 tbsp. flour with the sugar.

Different apples produce various grades of applesauce. The early summer green thin-skinned apples produce a very smooth, fine-textured, delicious applesauce.

Applesauce

Approximately 2 quarts

- 16-18 tart, unpeeled apples
- 1 cup water
- ½ cup sugar
- 2 tbsp. butter

Quarter apples, remove core and cut each piece again. Place apples and water in large pot and bring to a boil, stirring to prevent scorching. Reduce heat, and cook until apples are soft... from 20-40 minutes, stirring occasionally. If applesauce seems too thick, add more water; if too thin, cook longer to thicken. Put through a food mill, or sieve, and add butter. Add sugar gradually, tasting for desired sweetness.

continued....

If you want more zip, add some grated lemon rind and lemon juice, and/or some nutmeg or cinnamon, tasting as you add...or — stir in ½ cup raspberry juice for Raspberry Applesauce.

Raspberry Applesauce

   1 pint black raspberries
   ¼ cup water

Bring raspberries and water to a boil. Reduce heat and simmer 15-20 minutes, until raspberries are well cooked. Cool and strain thru cheesecloth.

This makes about ½ cup of juice and will keep in your refrigerator for over a week. Add to cooked applesauce, chill and serve. Particularly good served with pork.

Applesauce Meringue

Serves 6

- 4 cups applesauce
- 1 tbsp. lemon juice
- grated rind of 1 lemon
- 4 egg yolks
- 4 egg whites
- 8 tbsp. sugar
- ½ tsp. vanilla

Preheat oven 300°. Combine applesauce, lemon juice and rind. Beat in egg yolks and pour into baking dish. In separate bowl, beat egg whites until peaks form. Gradually add sugar while continuing to beat. Add vanilla. Mix approximately ¼ of meringue thru applesauce and spoon remaining meringue on top. Bake 15 minutes. Delicious hot or cold.

Warm applesauce — a nice change of pace in Winter... sprinkle cinnamon or nutmeg on top.

Apple Squares

½ cup butter or margarine
1 cup sugar
1 egg
1 cup flour
½ tsp. baking powder
¼ tsp. salt
2 apples, peeled and chopped
½ cup chopped nuts

Preheat oven 350°.
Cream butter and sugar and beat in egg. Combine flour, baking powder and salt and gradually add to butter and sugar mixture. Gently stir in apples and nuts, and spread in buttered 8"x 8" pan. Bake 35 minutes.

Au naturel! A bowl of chilled red and yellow apples makes a super Fall or Winter dessert... serve with fruit knives.

Baked Apples

Core...without cutting thru bottom of apple...and peel upper half of 4-6 baking apples. Place in baking dish. Preheat oven 375°. Fill center of each apple with brown sugar, dot with butter and sprinkle with cinnamon. Or...fill with your favorite preserves...apricot, marmalade, or whole cranberry sauce and a little brown sugar. Sprinkle with chopped nuts and pour ½ cup orange juice...or water...over apples. Bake 45 minutes or until apples are tender. Basting improves their flavor.

Apples Meringue

Beat 2 egg whites until peaks form. Gradually beat in 4 tbsp. sugar, continuing to beat until stiff. Add 1 tbsp. lemon juice. Pile meringue over baked apples and return to oven for another 5-8 minutes.

Ripe apples are firm, juicy and flavorful. Over-ripe apples lack flavor and become mushy when cooked. Certain varieties of apples are better for cooking than others, as they'll hold their shape. Ask your supplier.

Baked Apple Rings

    4 baking apples
    ½ cup brown sugar
    ½ tsp. powdered cloves
    ½ tsp. cinnamon
    ½ cup honey
    ½ cup water

Preheat oven 400°. Core and slice apples into ½ inch rings. Place in shallow baking dish. In saucepan, combine and heat remaining ingredients. Pour over apples and bake 15 minutes or until tender, turning to baste once or twice.

Date & Apple Squares

½ cup butter or margarine, softened
¾ cup sugar
1 egg
2 apples, peeled and finely chopped
½ cup chopped dates
½ cup chopped nuts
1½ cups flour
½ tsp. baking soda
1 tsp. baking powder

Preheat oven 350°. Blend butter and sugar, then beat in egg. Stir in apples, dates and nuts. In separate bowl, combine flour, baking soda and powder. Gradually stir into apple mixture. Spread in a greased 9"x9" pan and bake 30 minutes.

Easy Topping for apple desserts.
Blend 2-3 tbsp. applesauce and ¼ tsp. cinnamon with 8 oz. softened cream cheese.

Easy Apple Cake

Serves 4-6

4 apples, peeled and sliced
¼ cup sugar
½ tsp. cinnamon

½ cup sugar
2 tbsp. soft butter (margarine)
1 egg
¼ tsp. vanilla
1 cup flour
1 tsp. baking powder

Mix together ¼ cup sugar and cinnamon. Place a layer of apples in greased baking dish, sprinkle with half the sugar-cinnamon, cover with remaining apples and cover with remaining sugar-cinnamon. Preheat oven 350°. Cream ½ cup sugar and butter. Add egg and vanilla and mix well. Stir in flour and baking powder and spoon over apples, spreading as best you can. Bake 30 minutes.
Superb served warm, with vanilla ice cream.

Apple Scones

Makes about 18

2 cups flour
3 tsp. baking powder
2 tbsp. sugar
½ tsp. cinnamon
½ tsp. salt
6 tbsp. shortening
½ cup apples, peeled and finely chopped
½ cup raisins
cold apple juice, or milk ... about 4 tbsp.

Preheat oven 400°. Mix together dry ingredients. Cut in shortening as you would for pie crust. Stir in apples and raisins. Add enough juice to make a stiff dough. On floured surface, roll dough about ½ inch thick. Cut into triangles and bake on cookie sheet for 10 minutes, or until light brown.

Apple Butter

The thicker skinned, late Summer and Fall apples produce a grainier texture that's best for apple butter.

- 3 qts. unsweetened applesauce
- 2 lbs. granulated sugar
- 1 lb. brown sugar
- 3/4 cup apple cider

Stir ingredients together and cook in a slow oven...325°...for 3 hours, stirring occasionally. Add:

- 1/2 tsp. nutmeg
- 1/4 tsp. allspice
- 3/4 tsp. cloves
- 3 tsp. cinnamon

Return to oven and cook one hour more.

Apple butter requires long, slow cooking, which makes it a good candidate for a crockpot.

Apple Dip

    8 oz. cream cheese, softened
    ½ cup mayonnaise
    2 medium apples, chopped
    ½ cup chopped walnuts
    1 tbsp. lemon juice

Blend together cheese and mayonnaise. Add apples, nuts and lemon juice. Serve with crackers.

Easy Apple Relish

Makes 3½ cups

Cranberries and apples team up well together.

    2 cups fresh cranberries
    2 apples
    1 orange, peeled and seeded
    2 cups sugar

Finely chop...or grind cranberries, apples and orange. Mix with sugar and refrigerate for a day or two before serving. Great with chicken or turkey.

Honey Apples, for a side dish or dessert. Heat 1 cup honey and ½ cup vinegar. Peel and thinly slice 3 cups apples. Drop a few slices at a time into the simmering honey mixture and cook until tender.

Apple Fritters

Makes 12-15

1 cup flour
1 tsp. baking powder
¼ tsp. cinnamon

2 eggs
½ cup milk
2 apples, chopped

Mix dry ingredients. In separate bowl, beat eggs, stir in milk and apples. Combine with dry ingredients. Drop one tablespoonful at a time into hot...375°...fat. Fry until golden brown. Drain and serve sprinkled with confectioners' sugar, and/or maple syrup.

Apple Pancakes

Makes about 12

Light and delicious!

- 3 eggs, separated
- 3 tbsp. sour cream
- 1 peeled apple, finely chopped
- 3 tbsp. flour
- 1 tsp. baking powder
- ½ tsp. cinnamon

Separate eggs and add sour cream, apple, flour, baking powder and cinnamon to the yolks, stirring well. Beat egg whites until peaks form, and fold into yolk mixture. Cook on hot, lightly greased griddle until golden brown. Delicious served with a dollop of sour cream and maple syrup.

An apple is over 80% water, which makes it a great thirst quencher.

Peanut Butter & Apples

English Muffins
peanut butter
apple slices
brown sugar
cinnamon
bacon slices (optional)

Split muffins and lightly toast. Spread them with peanut butter and arrange apple slices on top. Sprinkle with sugar and cinnamon. Partially cook bacon, cut strips and place on top. Cook under broiler for a few minutes.

Apples, peaches, pears and plums are all members of the rose family. Apple blossoms greatly resemble the blossoms of the wild rose.

Apple Maple Stuffing

Great for a goose or a crown roast of pork.

- 1 stalk celery, chopped
- 1 medium onion, chopped
- 6 tbsp. butter or margarine
- 3 apples, chopped
- ¼ cup maple syrup
- ¾ cup water
- 4 cups herb-seasoned cubed stuffing mix

Simmer celery and onion in 4 tbsp. butter for 2 minutes. Add apples and remaining 2 tbsp. butter and simmer another 2 minutes. Add syrup and water and bring to a boil. Measure 4 cups stuffing mix into large bowl. Add hot mixture, stirring well. Enough for a 6-10 lb. bird.